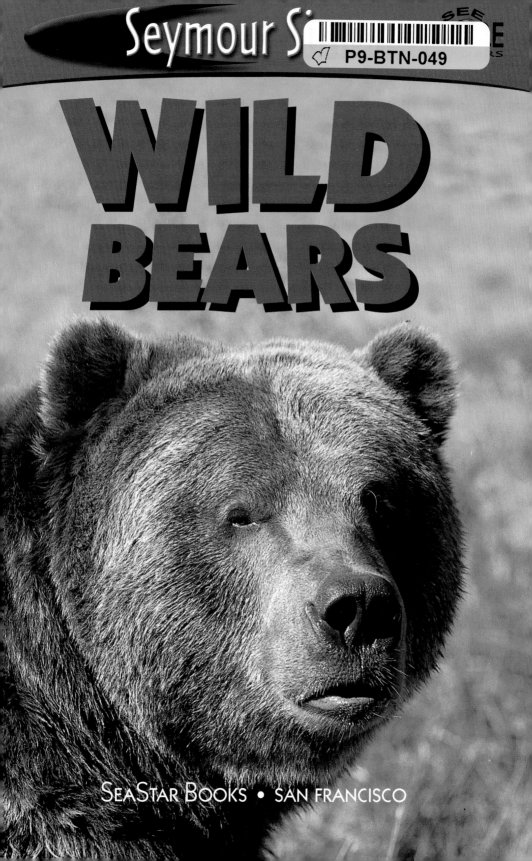

Seymour Simon

WILD BEARS

SeaStar Books • San Francisco

This book is dedicated to my grandson Benjamin.

Special thanks to reading consultant Dr. Linda B. Gambrell, Director of the School of Education at Clemson University, past president of the National Reading Conference, and past board member of the International Reading Association.

Permission to use the following photographs is gratefully acknowledged:
front cover, pages 8–11, 18–19, 32: © Jeff Lepore, Photo Researchers, Inc.; title page: © Renee Lynn, Photo Researchers, Inc.; pages 2–3: © Bruce Herman, Photo Researchers, Inc.; pages 4–5: © G. C. Kelley, Photo Researchers, Inc.; pages 6–7: © Stephen J. Krasemann, Photo Researchers, Inc.; pages 12–13: © Daniel J. Cox/naturalexposures.com; pages 14–15: © Leonard Lee Rue III, Photo Researchers, Inc.; pages 16–17: © Sylvain Cordier, Photo Researchers, Inc.; pages 20–21: © Pat & Tom Leeson, Photo Researchers, Inc.; pages 22–23: © Dan Guravich, Photo Researchers, Inc.; pages 24–25: © Tom McHugh, Photo Researchers, Inc.; pages 26–27: © John Giustina/Bruce Coleman, Inc.; pages 28–29: © Rob & Ann Simpson/Visuals Unlimited; pages 30–31: © Tim Davis, Photo Researchers, Inc.

ISBN 1-58717-144-9

SeaStar is an imprint of Chronicle Books LLC.

Library of Congress Cataloging-in-Publication Data is available.

Distributed in Canada by Raincoast Books
9050 Shaughnessy Street, Vancouver, British Columbia V6P 6E5

10 9 8 7 6 5

Chronicle Books LLC
85 Second Street, San Francisco, California 94105

www.chroniclekids.com

Bears live all over the world.

Bears are different colors

and different sizes.

Some bears are very large

and dangerous.

But other bears are not.

Bears are mammals, like dogs, wolves, and foxes.

Bears have strong bodies covered in thick fur.

They have short tails and long claws.

Most bears eat both animals and plants.

Bears can remember where they found food.

Bears have strong legs
and can run very fast.
Big grizzly bears
can charge at
30 miles
an hour.

A bear's face looks
a lot like a dog's face.
Bears do not have
good eyesight.
But they do hear well
and have a great sense
of smell.
Bears often raise their
heads and sniff the air
to check what
is around them.

In the winter, when there
is little to eat, a bear's
heart rate slows down.
It does not eat or drink.
A hibernating bear
can lose up to half of
its weight over the winter.

Most bears give birth to cubs in a cave, a hollow tree, or some other hidden place.

One to three cubs

are born at a time.

They have no fur and are helpless.

North American bear cubs are born in late January or February. The family leaves the den in late winter or early spring.

Bear cubs spend their first 18 months to three years with their mother.

There are seven

main types of bears.

Different kinds of brown bears

live in the northern parts of

North America, Europe, and Asia.

Kodiak bears of Alaska are

the largest bears in the world.

They stand ten feet tall and weigh

more than 1,000 pounds.

American black bears weigh
from 125 to 600 or more pounds
and are about six feet long.
Black bears aren't always black.
Their fur can be blue, tan,
or even white.
Asian black bears are smaller
than their American cousins.

Polar bears walk on top
of the Arctic ice and swim
in the freezing ocean waters.

A thick layer of fat keeps them warm.

Their favorite food is young seals.

They can kill a seal with a single

blow of a paw.

Sun bears are the smallest
of all the bears.

They weigh only 60 to 80 pounds.

Sun bears are sometimes called
"honey bears" because they like
honey so much.

They live in the rain forests
of Southeast Asia.

Sloth bears live in the forests
of India and Sri Lanka.
They use long, curved front claws
to dig up nests of termites.
Putting their faces into the nest,
they suck the insects into
their mouths through a gap
in their front teeth.

Spectacled bears are
the only bears that live
in South America.
They get their name from
the rings, or "spectacles,"
of light-colored fur
around their eyes.
Spectacled bears are
good climbers.
They eat mainly fruits
and nuts.

Giant pandas eat bamboo stalks and leaves in the jungles of western China. Pandas eat up to 60 pounds of bamboo each day. Pandas are also the star attractions in some zoos.

When people cut down forests, they force out bears and other animals living on wild land. If we want to have bears in nature, we need to leave a home for them. The future of bears is up to us.